Buying the Farm

also by Eliza O'Toole

The Dropping of Petals
A Cranic of Ordinaries

Buying the Farm

(a georgics of sorts)

Eliza O'Toole

Shearsman Books

First published in the United Kingdom in 2025 by
Shearsman Books Ltd
PO Box 4239
Swindon
SN3 9FN

Shearsman Books Ltd Registered Office
30–31 St. James Place, Mangotsfield, Bristol BS16 9JB
(this address not for correspondence)

www.shearsman.com

EU AUTHORISED REPRESENTATIVE:
Lightning Source France
1 Av. Johannes Gutenberg, 78310 Maurepas, France
Email: compliance@lightningsource.fr

ISBN 978-1-84861-982-1

Copyright © Eliza O'Toole, 2025

The right of Eliza O'Toole to be identified as the author of this work has been asserted by her in accordance with the Copyrights, Designs and Patents Act of 1988. All rights reserved.

NO AI TRAINING
Without in any way limiting the author's and publisher's exclusive rights under copyright, any use of this publication to "train" generative artificial intelligence (AI) technologies to generate text is expressly prohibited. The author reserves all rights to license uses of this work for generative AI training and development of machine learning language models.

Cover image by the author © Eliza O'Toole

Contents

All a felt / 13
Field (n.)(v.) / 14
On fairy rings / 15
In the season of sowing barley / 16
Dip-tailed ouzeling / 17
Feeding on flowers / 18
Farming the last year / 19
Mythology can ask / 20
The severalls, yardlands and oxgangs overcome / 22
Stigma / 23
In alto-rilievo; it is necessary to be prophetic / 24
The alienation / 25
I felt a funeral in my brain; in a dominating style, he was painted / 27
Debitage / 28
Thallic / 29
Swallow day, the summer meeting of
swallows and crows in the tithe-barn / 30
Futhorc / 31
Participial and Perfective; the grammar of the valley prefixed / 32
Swallow holes, or the arrival of swallows and the removal of tombs / 33
The rising and falling of valley fields / 34
Cloud formations / 35
Being arable, bone assemblages, a burying / 36
Being on an eyot in the floodplain of the Stour;
by way of raised causeway / 37
All our hills were tangled wood / 38
Within reach, a lamb's tale / 39
The Red Massey Ferguson / 40
When the wind is right / 41
Slip face / 42
Booms Prayers / 43
Unless you run your Head into a Hedge / 44
Abscission / 45
Exiguus mus – a georgic / 47

Degrees of Calling / 48
Consumptive / 49
Loom weight / 50
Cutting greens / 51
Barn-dust / 54
The first cut / 55
Naming of grass / 56
Wrung a warrening / 58
From the frogbit, pleiades / 59
Farmed out: a georgic for the depleting of seeds / 60
Geometrical omissions / 61
Counting crows / 62
Strong chemicals, wet harvest / 63
The formation of abscission layers / 64
Thin alluvium, becoming field, or Everything Rises / 65
Corpse coins, becoming green / 66
In between the in between / 67
The Geometrical Swelling of Yellow; the invention of the umbrella / 68
The drawing of words; sermons in (mill)stone / 69
Spawning; the ghost in the field at dusk / 70
New full dew pond / 71
Unstable dispersions / 72
Slant cubitus / 73
In trinities, the building of permanent things
when time is impermanent / 74
Holding on / 75
A catechism on supposition / 76
Breaking bones, ~~on being aloof~~ / 77
Unhistorical acts / 78
Caterpillars' evolution / 79
Suitable pins to pin your Heart Moth / 80
A kind of wasp / 81
Unthankful villages / 82
The Golden Promise; embryo rescue and the multiplicities of
many-rowed malting barleys / 83
The Seven Pillars of Pesticide / 84
Adderbolts gaping / 85

after-ripening / 86
The (mis)timing of Summer / 87
Crowsticks; congregations with bells / 88
Food plants / 89
Bringing in the green / 90
Heritage / 92
Hunting / 93
Belief in evergreens / 94
The underside of leaves / 95
Farm accounting / 96
On coming to a standstill / 97
Church accounting – Blessed are the Birds psalm 84:3 / 98
Still, Life / 99
Earth-movers / 100
For the unadulterated lex loci or the tout ensemble / 101
Announcement of domain, counting tweets / 103
Und leuchtet wie die Sonne /
Matris in gremio. / Alpha es et O. / / 104
Tax Collection / 105
A divinity of bees / 106
Xylogenesis, an (Edenic   ) fall / 107
High Site Fidelity / 108
The pastoral side / 109
Occurrences in Fields / 110
A distraction of congregations; on the wall porphyry is red / 111
Simultaneous; black henbane, the eroding edge of empire / 112
Domestication / 113
Being the shepherd, having hard hooves and easy lambing traits / 114
The maples are in full flame, hedges flaring / 115
Gall, or on never eating blackberries after Michaelmas Day / 116
Ordinary; left over from butchery / 117
Intonation of generations of cattle-droving two centuries ago / 118
A de-composition / 119
Seeing Blue / 121
Bi O ptics / 122
Field (playing the) / 123
Collective motion, or winter grazing of a fresh field of vetch / 124

Hockets / 125
Ancestries / 126
R a v e n / 127
Coming back to land / 128
Weeping Hill; to be exactly placed, disinheriting perspectives / 129

Notes / 130
Acknowledgements / 135

A (Modern) Pastoral

'Every furrow owns a land.'
—John R. Stilgoe

'then came rigid iron and the melodious saw-blade'
—Virgil, *Georgics*, Book I

'Whoever could make two ears of corn, or two blades of grass, to grow upon a spot of ground where only one grew before, would deserve better of mankind, and do more essential service to his country, than the whole race of politicians put together.'
—Jonathan Swift, *Gulliver's Travels*

'Agriculture, the art in which nine-tenths of the capital of civilized nations is embarked, upon which all depend for subsistence, is rising towards its proper rank as a science. We look forward to the time when it will be generally conducted upon fixed and scientific principles, dependent upon immutable laws'
—James F. W. Johnston Edinburgh 1st February 1844.

For my Dad, who in a letter published in *The Times* in the early 1970s when it was broadsheet of repute, said, "The judge sits in the interests of law, the jury in the interests of justice. Were it not so one might well find the latter immaterial, irrelevant and incompetent before the majesty of the former." If he were alive we would agree that just as there is no justice in law, there is nothing natural in Nature, and farming is the original sin. Long live farming. RIP Dad.

Poet's Note

The phrase 'to buy the farm' is a euphemism for death. Attested etymologically at least to WWII. The term to 'buy it' means to die, the reference to 'farm' relating to the Anglo-Saxon *feorh* signifying life.

The word 'georgic' comes from the Greek for *earth*, the word means '*farming*'. It also means 'poem of rural or agricultural life' from the 1510s. The title of Virgil's poems on rural life is from the Greek '*geogikos*' meaning 'agricultural' with the root of '*gē*' meaning '*earth*', as in '*Gaia*'.

The root of the word 'farm' is rent from the Latin *firmare* meaning fixed payment for a specific tract of land, or – perhaps – the root of the word 'farm' is from Old English words that relate sound to sense, and so is rooted in the Anglo-Saxon word *feorh* meaning life.

From an Old English perspective, there has always been poetry in farming, and farming in poetry. And life and death in both.

All a felt
(on being georgic)

This is laden land. Heavy with Spring. This land yoked to legacy; flint bound in gravel sands. This lavender land, blue with bees, strewn with visionaries, with myth, and with apocryphal histories.

This is ald-land, grass-land broken up. Addling with barley-birds germinating in the season of sowing barley over-watched from high tops, dry with bald antiquity. This is coney-land, flint locked on talc and spar; *here with* an arrow and a bow, the crow-keeper battling new-sown land sour ploughed out with two rabbits and a knife.

Field (n.) (v.)

Abscission: a process of shedding, a cutting a part, a falling and a landing.

Possession: a conclusion of law, a defining of the nature of a particular relationship of control. Demonic over land. Reified.

Land (v.): a muddle, a rooted place, a willing coalition of living. & the dead.

Land (n.): there is no such thing.

Cleavage: state of being cleft, being divided by force, state of separation. Land after law.

Language: a set of words set upon sand conveying dominion of land. A maker of myth.

Lore: vernacular of the commons, before subjection by acquired language. When *questio quid juris* was irrelevant. When all lore was one lore.

Law: an originary violence and legitimating force in the name of a right. A holder of mythologies, a faker of truth made of (mis)histories. A contour of power, black letters, dead hand of, makes words binding.

Poetry: a naming and a making of names, an intercellular bridge, a disassembly, an unlimiting undeconstructible justice. Includes the non-human. Binds words together.

On fairy rings
(a field guide)

This scraped furze-land flecked with fox-torn down of February rabbits, and ringed green sour ragged with esculent fungus, grows cyanide –

and in the thin grass of this worked out sand-pit slope, the soil is hydrophobic, the grass desiccated, and the pollarded oaks are in decline.

In the season of sowing barley

come the barley-birds gathering in germinations and in the chamblings slight chicked in damp margins blown with blackthorn blossom slung among brauches of hazel-tails and brakes blown sideways in bossoching gales. These low fields fast overflown, clagged with freshes, bright vocal with March-birds, drain sod slow.

Dip-tailed ouzeling
(how to regain territory)

        these blackbirds break the night

        singing territory into right, these
        dawn the dusk warrioring and
        worming above the slight greening
        hagaþon, lungs liquid littering the
        span of March fullsong with Spring

        daffodils dog-pee gold bend low
        bird beak-colour or goslin yellow,
        and in a black gliff of quackles, with
        a fast bow and a run, casts off in a
        brash-flash of dip-tailed rattocking

Feeding on flowers

it was all rainbows and crowtoes, the river up rose and risen was a misplacement of sprung green submerged and low ground swallowing. It was prime and the drowned were firstlings of Spring, and all the shadows geniculate and long purpling

awkward the equinox sun, a root day, perresil sprouting toward a lambing storm, this blackthorn winter blowing following borrowed days, fleet until the soil stays warm

Farming the last year
(tenurial)

It was the blue that wasn't there, it was the day ploughed out, this field ended, shadows wide open, yellow belly distended. It was the tractors red and green patterning flint full land right up the edge, and the hare stone still in the sedge by the ditch, the water

                    still

                            coursing.

Mythology can ask
('to make two blades of grass to grow where only one grew before.')

       seed and a garden begins / with a seed which is like a memory / which like a seed grows / and if it's a bad seed / *who knows* / a memory can be made to grow as can seeds if the rain is right and the temperature is right and it's the right time with the right light and everything coalesces into the just right tightness for the carapace to crack and then / right out / it seeps

it is through cracks that things leak / *what things* / things with wings / diptera and wingless things with leaves, dicotyledons, stigma-stuck frass / seeping into cracks where little things creep and rain gets in – and mythology

still the rain gets in and out comes a sprout, glinting frailest of unfastenings unflattening/ emarginate carapace

burst under slant weathering and syntax, slender deportment / picking out space / *who knew why* / and above / sky – glimmering. Then the crack / lightning's haze grazing the gloaming and then carmine red slicing flint

a part split pod, slit seeded as clouds bearing rain, striated incus thunder headed dripping till the fissure fills picking out calved words god-like, and verily / like in myths / Thor spitting tacks stark tracks back to violet / slate-magenta / green and various shades of dirty Prussian blue

still the sprout, tongue like bifurcating dialogue between embryo and in endosperm, a germ of a memory, lodged in a split / transient / cleaved and activated / *what by or by what* / as sudden as that and everything coalesces

everything begins with embryonic development and a molecular dialogue between / in the crack, seepage and cuticle formation after cleavage / cotyledons after cleft / after pattern formation / after zygotic genome activation / and after / shimmer in the dew and shiver through chlorophyll accumulation / a wild type crossing and zygotic elongation cascade / like memories in the Spring, signalling

a mythology / begins / transcript carryover of maternal origin beginning with a seed which is like a memory which like a seed grows / and grows / sometimes in rows always proper embryos / globular heart torpedoes and then / unbending green / nascent cotyledon

and a body plan / myth laden / thus grows memory unfading and expressed a Titaness / latent with tissue patterning, epigenetic mucilage and metabolites apically seeking the sky / pitter pattering / for curse and glory, only who knows the truth / of the myth of the *how* that might signify / not the husk of a who / but the raw-blood sponge-full fat wet-red marrow / of the *why*

The severalls, yardlands and oxgangs overcome
(*becoming vast*)

                        in the aftermath of flowers, Spring showers and hares glinting like wet lead cower in the furrows, beached by plough clearance and left overs from high yielding crops. These shear-bolted mould-board heavies don't jump; these inverting tines plough once and run right through.

Stigma
(sticking-place, a day for the making of nails)

Reverberant was the morning, massive with bees after rain, upending blackthorn blossom insistenting a liturgical refrain. Everything was unusual, affodilling into April, and Fin and I were wading the endlessness of green when a slew of sudden starlings murmuring a Fibonacci curve furled and we saw cast a sodden sheep, old struggling. We right the sheep. A pregnant ewe. It was a medieval common pasture, then Norman brick on Roman herringbone. It was still, it was late March and there was rain on couchant carved stone. There were crows. It was good Friday.

In alto-rilievo; it is necessary to be prophetic
(*the routeing of roots*)

So was the quickening of Spring, the hedges were thickening, the ants were on the march. Red kites and green helicopters were isomorphic in the sky. And choreographic – were alienating the apocalyptic sublimity of a panoramic easter day. It was the crows congregating in the oaks, the same lingering rain, and it was the same dim-lit centuries ingrained. It was Saxon, then Norman, all underpinned with Roman set astride the pagan, and then it was attacking sledge-hammering under reforming royal ordering with much later restoring. Then after uncovering, it was Victorian and recovered up with wax. It was a clearing, an inhabiting, and it was lost pet rabbits in the graveyard, a sermoning St. Francis and a tourmaline dragon liturgically misplaced.

The alienation

A parenthesis of thin flailed raw lane edging hedges making an oblong of wind-swept piss yellowing late winter grass, metribuzin, flufenacet and diflufenican sprayed, a field.

Metabolic resistance built up by black grass wild oats rye grass chickweed & mayweed to oil dispersed mesosulfron and iodosulfron.

Act of estranging, disowning. To part with.

To treat as a stranger. This land doesn't remember. Grass pollen carried on the wind.

To separate; people from place, ecosystem from land, self-regulation from second nature. Broken ground, grammar less, unphrased, uprooted.

A transfer of title to land from one to another, to part with land. To become departed. Conveyed away.

Muddled corners of fields, beyond the reach of boom sprayers, huddled rabbit eyes ooze puss, too slight to flee, pants gently. The crows flare.

To break away. Quarried. Ectopic.

That can be given up.

Alius; another, other, different *from* al "beyond"

Detached, detourned, a predicament of attachments, the splitting of postmitotic sisters

and ingression of the cleavage furrow and partitioned

between being there and not there, plein air, not a where, a what, an awareness of that
wet scent of rain, cedar, propolis, a queen supine, warm wax and wormwood, mist rising
between the bee and the tree, here

an acre

turned over, wallowed pasture grass made cash,   a hypothermic matted grey rabbit

separate, still

breathing   stares,   white blinded.

I felt a funeral in my brain; in a dominating style, he was painted
(the servants of Sir Richard Waldegrave who owns the land haunted by the dragon came forth to shoot it with arrows …almost the whole county was summoned to slaughter it but when it saw that it was to be shot at again, it fled to the marsh, hid in the reeds and was seen no more)

It was a medieval tympanic of a morning and over leaf, the sky was black and blue and the amuletic lilacs were scent-filling out with rain. And the dragon was red with tourmaline and the boys were in pickling barrels and part of the Body at the passion was missing and with the apostles feet, a beheading (the Baptist) and all were mainly illegible and all smelt faint-wet of echo and damp. And under the Victorian mortar, and after much restoring, and by way of the Norman vestry, the Romans still remain.

Debitage

(*in an effort to obtain dates*)

It happed after, that vpon the buryels grewe a right fayre flouredelyse. It was at that place, after that, this place of biriel, anabatrum, in a byryelle, a chyrchestyle where Fin and I sat sepulchrum in the braddle of spearing æsc watching bottle-toms barrelling and blowan flowering when we heard the sharp clear sound of a medieval mouth harp. It was after that, in the wellynge up and then the havocking of a whipped line of frothy spring limes and a disturbance of guinea fowl, it was after that, patinated flake scars, old fractures and bone refitting; and after that, it was hammered, it was a tractor's ditch of lithic flint and reassembling, it was a babbling river and spillings of scillingas and not long after that, it was a field spread flock of metal detectorists history-haunting.

Thallic

(*sprouting green*)

The sky sprung, the low field all sogges and sinks and after wholly spating is slowly draining. Fin is up to his belly and I, overtopped in my wellies, am flailing. Ancient, the crowtoes crowding wood anemones raise wet blue, and the sky squat is set to sprynge this remnant wild wood garlic white. Shearing all over, we are slight cant, creaking in the squeaking bright of the upward thrust of sprouting thallic green. The plank bridge has sunk, Fin puts a brace of mallards to flight. On the horizon, a tractor, crab-harrowing.

Swallow day; the summer meeting of swallows and crows in the tithe-barn
(Hirundo, hirundinaria and the spreading of celandines)

It was that, cockshut time, and the crows were going over. Below, abandoned plants growing wild and celadonite, were yellow-eyed and closing. Hedge-full, swallow-struck vnder the shaddowes of the ashe tree this swalowe affronting the sky ends Spring crevassing the swolowys grownde vorago riding thermals and downwash, tipping vortices and climbing kinematically fork-tails a foraging turn frontal into the wind straight diving bill-full to tight tithe-barn holes brimful of witch-chicks swart-stark and blind eyed to their medieval kin in the old settling of the same dusking of the same corn-gold Somer making.

Futhorc
(*ridge reading for roots*)

That. *And here I hear the fowlis synge.* Hear. That. The ridge rooked, the āc tip greening sepulchral-vast skeletal slant-leans against the sky. One scant leaf at a time, one slight, one greening, the spreading of the first foliar flush, an old word long on roots demarcating the drove-way agin the headland a revenanting of the ragged remnant of once-was wildwood, a ridge so left in the body of the valley, a drift, wood-sorrel, fine wild garlic, soft shoots, a belling stag, high is the sun, and in the blostmum and in originall tongues, deer still stalking.

Participial and perfective; the grammar of the valley prefixed
(the fastening of things, or it was more than that)

Brackly rain is ringing the pond, that lilac in full purple, that gale shrill, horizontal the hail sheet-beating the corrugating, and ruthfulling hamorian the flowering cherries, wild whip-lashed. In the field a tide of barley deening was rolling and high resurging. That the knowing of the growing was in the ground, that the addling of roots was in the shoots rising, and that the inclementing of the wide green late spring winds were resounding an ocean, that the valley cleaved and silence followed and the ghost ponds arisen were swallow heaved, and the crows unflapping were flowing over, and rooks were rough ruckling in the oaks, that should be enough.

§wallow holes, or the arrival of swallows and the removal of tombs

(at Burum an ancient royal hill, the known bound between East Essex and Suffolk, a barn-chapel to swallows in the corn, a cracked sarcophagus in the wood, an engraved death slab prostrate by the bins in a back garden)

§ That clattered the hail through glowering Payne's grey and icy striated incus, the entire sky blown over having seen this tight mown consecrated ground, this engraved head and breathing stone, and over leaf the dragon curling shadowed in green sward over which a buzzard hurling much as when the dank mere mirror shone alchemically with sharp Aprilling rain consecrating again this wind shrill land. Still standing here narrating are the interminable ghosts of a martyr-king and a cardinal, slight worn scant edged, mote dusting red iridescence in the cirrus curling of royal blue aslant effigies, thin threads of liturgie and a long line of mediaeval dynasty documenting the ten crisp centuries of the Manorial dead. Arcing archaically wings narrowed arrow over-head barn-swallows are still arriving §§§

The rising and falling of valley fields
(the ploughing out of this well-versed land)

That standing on the headland, this ground in old language, carlicks, warlock, wild mustard, poverty weed, coltsfoot and fat hen stretching acres of centuries and fag ends of ryegrass and wild oats, stover left over from the nineteen thirties, haysel fled in the flashing out of brews where knotgrass grew cursed and the sky was sparse. This land sheared down the valley side fleet furrowed under plough on and off for five centuries or longer, buck-headed the hedges, the rank odour of elder overlaying the scouring hagabon and crouching under, the hare in its form, and an excarnation of crows in flapping rows, clawing skyward. Under-foot tanged-and-barbed arrowheads, sherds and tegulae; aftermath, and above, arriving screaming, the develin.

Cloud formations
(without the dreams of birds, would we be dreamless?)

It was a morning irreducible to things. The birds were sermoning and the hail was roaring down the valley horizontally followed by rain and in the suddening of gusts it was hurling hedge blossom petals, sodden and adhering to the green of the streaming dreams of crows claw curling in the still bare branches of the ebbles cracking back above the rippling blue of the bells in the gale, and the tawnies forebrained were haunting. They were a crucible, ancestrally still and in the āc, deep sleeping.

Being arable, bone assemblages, a burying
(recovering a plot, the then maintenance of fertility in fields)

This, that manuring scatters, this medieval drove way, that heavy land mould-board ploughed out sheared and recoiled headland soil, those walking dung machines arable expanding and woodland clearing. Those felled bone pathologies proxied for traction mixed with sheep's bones proxied for shit shepherded and mixed with weed seeds, pollen cored, spring sown barley grains and charred plant remains, remain a seaming repository of the enclosing fields of a strata of the compression of time, yielding a soft body for the long storing or fast burying of the mythos of a grazed and hard gardened Eden.

Being on an eyot in the floodplain of the Stour; by way of raised causeway
(Est Engle was, as Abbo Cernuus describes it in the tenth Century, 'washed by waters on nearly every side')

That it was forest clad, was ancienting, was tine bellowing and is now missing from maps, this that was chief quarry, that this wood was building stone, this that stone full eyot, consecrating mound, moat wound around, lain under by septarian flint-stone ice-posited in boulder clay. That there are shells and fishes in the stones, that wholly explained by flood. You see water, you see wood, (they say) that heaven be no safer than the earth, (they say) giants piled mountains up to the stars and (they say) earth drenched, was streaming with blood. And following flooding, the sceaf and the blood, a red Massey Ferguson and the headland's asquint with the scudding scour of seventy horse powers with replaceable shins, six shear fixed-furrow hitched and clogged hauling upland for the ploughing.

All our hills were tangled wood
(each one dwelling in the midst of one's own occupying)

persisting, this place, the Spring was late, the frost at furst, it held. The morning was right arly, was sometime past April on the way to May, the hagabon was yetnot thick, right frawn it were and the plower were stopped and stick ont slant row along the vallie slope. The plowers they made long furrows here for all those years, holl centuries, long furrows in the fallow feld land, same midden hidden as graves lain side by side, god's acre wholly riddled and now risen up, all that earth, these hills, this tangled wood, all those guts & bones, this horizontal headland creased and slit, all that plower power still besprecan.

Within reach, a lamb's tale
(spatially demonstrative, the propensity of jackdaws to give)

A jackdaw drops this / wrong orange bright ringed at my feet in the rain-cast iridescent dawn washed green of vasts and slews of slant waves of fading blues and of Spring's decline / a string of soft straggling, long thin of lanolin, a lamb bereft of tail / the bones feel fused, cold and hard, the new wool coated like wax with wet, the rain repelled. Fin, expectant. This that and buttercups, this bedraggling of just grown fallen bone / set this alone, and all this that can be seen, this disarticulation of tails, that bird wrought, yellow buttercups and the incessant green / this that we call ours.

The Red Massey Ferguson
(for William Carlos Williams)

About that. This red wheel in the sky. Barrowing along the upland. Roaring horses powering the disk harrow, sudden glory in the morning. A red Massey Ferguson flashing in the sun upon which so much depends.

When the wind is right
(*the land strikes out*)

                          a kind of crop, these stones, this land littered with flint, with origins and occasional hells, with slight flares of prickling verticals spring green spiking through the sand shifting scaldy land sourced and sliced with rivulets undercutting brick-red in the running of the Aprilling rains. This land slides, and when the wind is right, between the gas guns and the Massey Ferguson, Fin and I fugitive footpathing, hear the first calling cuckoo carving out the hereditary from the wind-blown silt and grit of this obliterating territory.

Slip face

it was a stone & then it was an
abstraction of standing

it was the flaking of flint
& the sparks lit by it

it was the skin, thin with it
stretched over &
particulate

it was wind brimming & it was
hard silicious driving rain
inarticulate

it was the land & then it was an
abstraction of property

it was the movement of glaciers & then

when

the mountain intervened

it was sand

Booms Prayers

('And towering weeds malignant shadows yield; / And spreading succory chokes the rising field') — Virgil, Georgics, Book I

in the small-leaved limes' first leaves, swarming scent, and how to revive the declining bees. And in the fields waterlogging and winter wheat slight spike emerging, green through root sloshed rain-washed pre-emergence herbicide and swell-full anaerobic soil clogging stunted root growth. And on the wind, strong chemistry, methyl sodium mixings and flufenacet to control the Spring, the boom sprayers prayers for the sheen of all that new de-grassed bottle-glass green

Unless you run your Head into a Hedge
(if you walk)

wearing into the sunshine, two earth-boards, and a double-backed share-beam. And at the start of an elm, buttercups and in the field cows among calves and steers, pollen rubbing yellow onto udders, paigles, may buds, king cups, and cuckoo-bud, teacups, butter-flower, soldier buttons and toad tether, mud gold urea sprinklings, dung sun of centuries, for as long as there have been cows in meadows, for as long as there are cows, cattle on these deep kneed feeding grounds, these further than eyes can see, glazed and shining with high tides of small faced deep rooted tuberous creepings, will species forever these meadows with yelwe rides of piss gold crazy grazings.

Abscission

I

I remember the heat and the cows, and the shimmers in between, and the cows' pats and their halos of flies, their crusts, and the warm belch of the dairy herd, all piss and shit. I remember the field, the divots and the sandy soil, the places where limbs lay fallen and the nettles, the damp depressions puddled by the herd, the rings of field mushroom the size of plates under the drip line of the big old horse chestnuts, the drunken estate railings. I remember chewing the soft white inner stems at the base of blades of lime green grass, the sweet sheath shared with the deep cherry Lincolnshire Reds; and having stung legs spiked by scratchy pasture. I remember blood. I remember Pat the Polish cowman, and his skinny sheep dog. There were no sheep, but Jess brought up the Reds for milking and they were as meek as sheep under her stare. I remember the dairy clock striking every quarter, five minutes before the church chimed. Five minutes gave the dairy herd time to be there, ready to start the milking hour. I remember the Reds swishing their tails in the dry, and the dust and the flies, and I remember the long slow, the dust motes float, and that it was five o'clock. I remember the tinder grass and high summer. The glimmer and the stink. I remember the telephone wires stretched to infinity, the thrum of endless fields of harrowed furrows. And the bombing swallows. Screaming. Sky full.

II

I remember deep damp ditches, dogwood, spindle, guelder rose, wild damson, cherry plum, crab apple, oak and ivy and my bare arms clawed by blackthorn whilst looking for wild garlic, bluebells, and Queen Anne's lace. I remember the grubbing out of hedges, the gashes, the gaping holes with trashed raw edges. I remember the stumps grinding and the chain saws. Sappy and whining. And at harvest, I remember with stricken awe, the miles and miles of burning straw. I remember streaming eyes, and the stranding: rabbits, hares, stoats, field mice. The stubble burning, the flickers of sparks and the glittering glimmerings of moths smoking. I remember choking, and the sloughing skies of pewter stoked with pink. And the shadow of a dog fox cresting the fire driven across acres and acres of smouldering stalks. And the diving pipistrelles. Echo locating. Sky full.

III

I remember the autonomous reality of the land and the loss of adhesion in the abscission layer. I remember the time of separation; I remember the fall.

Exiguus mus – a georgic
(winnowing & the garnering of gathered grains against the rain)

the rain rolls tympanic insisting on the polytunnel, bending Tyrian tips poking from the first bristlings of (blessed) thistles, elderflowers wide umbelling parasol-pour spray weighted onto up-shooting goose-grass, and sag. All those verticals horizontal. Under plastic the garlic grows, the beans broaden under towers of flowers heavy with bees, the carrots in sand head south as thin and pale as tails, under the strawberries in full rose, rows of double cotyledons on slight stems lush in symphony. The freesias last yellow scent is heaven sending. And wigwammed peas are starting to furl curls in tight Fibonacci rings. Rootling, the imponderable mouse still winnowing Eleusinian wicker ware, unsows rows and rows of French radish seeds. She'll cache them all away from here en masse, where no-one is farming the Spring

Degrees of Calling

(*this iridescence, this interference, this intensity of colour with angle change, this that most hunted bird in the world*)

That the dusk deeps with the bleating of lambs, blackbirds in heaps of leaves up end for snails. That in the finding of broken things: streptomycin phial necks, wings, tesserae and bedsprings with coiled earthworms, soiled and resting, sacral bones withheld unbranched and besides that the Cathayan bird, red-eyed wattling and following the bent stalked track of the displacing rain, more hunted than hawking harriers, and slight stepping that splintered glass forages the warreners makings. That this disyllabic crow call turns flint flake and chert towards the glowering west, that this rising deci-second flight call, that this barred iridescent sheen, bottle green in soaking late sprung grass, that tucket cucket tuck-e-tuck trisyllabic hiss that this dissonance that this Roman copper bird starts hard, that spark lit this, that whirred of spilt harmonic that *this* is spontaneous.

Consumptive

(apothecary bottles and the discommodities of the soyle)

myrie soyle, extractive of roots, smashed black coffin glass the cordial balm of Gilead, health restorer, our narrow and fowle lanes, our manifold inclosures, severed with so many deep ditches, ealdan heges, and store of wood, bushes and trees, the impassablenesse, so many bottles of poison, vulcanite stoppers and fractures of blue edge sharpening fields, dispensed of liniment, stone jars kiln-burned shouldering Darby's Carminative unearthed green with laudanum and after rain, soil borne tuberculin bacterium mixing with Mother Siegel's curative, surrounding ground arisen sentinel, tip chipped angel leaking hypodermic isoniazid

Loom weight

(Moat, medieval. Square with enclosures, wet – creek connecting to the Stour. Part occupied, hall. Adjoins church. Early Saxon fragment from features – medieval – eroding on moat edge, unshorn sheep bleating, wet buttercups, dung folded)

wool is come home, and is sorted, saymed, what with breakers, dyers, wood setters, wringers, spinners, weavers, burlers, sheersmen of all sorts and carriers. This wool they make vnto many severall purposes, being washed, scoured, kembed and trimmed, they putt it outt to spinning, of which they make a line thred according to the sort of the wool, of these spinners, that the gaine of this worke is so advantageable and cleanly in respect of the spinning, this that was so vncleane, so laboursome, and with so smal earning and for that they have more which offer themselves than there can att all times be worke provided for, now when their wooll is made into yarne, for the fleece is fine and the cheifest weight ariseth from flockes of sheep outt here on the heath and barren on champion hanging hunk dank, damp and bound, shreds, barbed wire wound around, shorn now of its old wealth, these deep dung full little lanes still frothy and sheep woven.

50

Cutting greens
(a checklist)

Appendant, the tractor, to the land, spreading pelleted fertiliser before the rain, adjusting appurtenance. Antientest. A second mowing, a second crop sown and reaped after harvest. Aftermath.

Bote by right before baling green in black plastic, fresh pasture.

Customarily contiguously chuff-cut commonables for feed fermenting, sheep couchant, the required remaining. Clamp busting (Acre Pack). Off the commons, commoners.

De facto. De-parked. Demesne (woodland). Following the drafting of ewes for regulation, by drove, divisio. Dogstail and dew on fences at dawn.

Estovered. Emparked. Ewes returned to common. Essential muck machines, an eclogue of sorts.

Fennaging fallow arables, fridaye pondes, and fold-closed fields, de-feoffed. First cut of grass up to Lammas day. Forage Express Grass (Five Acre Pack) fescue and fly-time.

Grazes the sheep walk this stinted grass, medium green and gaited. Goitrogenic meadow hay fed parenterally. Good grass apparently. Gainsboroughesque.

Half a year land, heafed the flock and hurdles hefted. Of wood, hazel and hawthorn. Of harvested haylage, grazing aftermath thereafter. Off the heath, heathens.

In-gross disattaching, here *wheare most inclosures be*.

Jure, de. The JCB forking rolling bales to waiting trailers.

Keep for the cows. Kernels of wheat. Off keltered the rake kit-cat belly rolling.

Leys, herbal, learing and hefting.

Multi Strike Grass Seed Mix (Ten Acre Pack). Barclamp, astoncrusader, kirial, tetragraze. Pushing hard with added nitrogen. Dynamic, established. Best cut high and four over. Mirror rights in common. Marled and muck spreading. Mange.

Nitrates, running off to ditches, cattle ruminating.

Old-fashioned permanent pasture grass seed mix (Twenty Acre Pack). Laura, Liherold, Lofa festulolium, Evora smooth stalked, Solo rough stalked, crested Dog and Timothy. Adaptable to changing climaticals.

Piscary, profit a prendre, pannage, prescription and pasturage. A little pecie of pightle, ealden heged.

Quasi-rights in common, *pari-pasu*. Peat defeated.

Rough stalked meadow grass (Thirty Acre Pack). Rams sold. Root riddled soil mattocked. Rotations.

Strip, an acre of land, furlonged and thin, a selion song of the outfield, and the sulh-sulh of the sevensteche plough, furrowing flat parallel arable soil. Shakes the field with the sound of four-footed. Smooth-stalked meadow grass (Forty Acre Pack). Shorn.

Teag, a close or enclosure in the sense of common pasture, now tye raising the past vast across the Essex/Suffolk clayland hundreds.

Unthrifty the lambs, rumen deflated.

Valleyed this place, sacred, a river running through, stourish. Virgilian.

Wains of hay crossing millponds, shallowing. Wagons should roll slow over flat fords, pitch forking. Wethers castrated and lambs weaned. Special wicker tools and winnowing fans used.

Xanadu, here were forests ancient as the hills. Here a fragment surrounded twice by five miles of fertile ground and sinuous rills, curdled.

Yeanlings on yardland belong to the fold, *soca falde*, cullet or no.

Zea, the stoutest of grass, oldest fodder grain in the world.

Barn-dust; odonata darting

(being mercurial)

It was this, dust-lifting. And there was no kicking out of the clods. The lizards moving like running water, the southern hawkers rising soft skinny from the pond, bullrush clasping to a slow hardening in the sun.

It was the motes and the dayflying moths revealing and the swallows streaming. Hay making in the clatter of birds and in the interstices and long roots, it was a latch lifting.

It was the rickling of damp-heat haze, a rusting blade and a blaze of flint. The rattling of the drive-train tractor trailers following the flail, it was the moisture sensing flake by flake and the high-density bales, the sharp as steel & hard teeth-cut.

It was cut after cut, net after net wrap loaded, hawking harriers following the shawm, roiling off the bouncing rig. And it was the dust motes and the dayflying moths revealing, and the swallows screaming. It was the southern hawkers rising soft skinny from the pond, it was odonata darting, grasping at the interstices and in the long roots a latch was lifting. And there was no kicking out of the clods.

The first cut
(cecini pascua, rura, ~~duces~~ - I have sung pastures, farms, ~~leaders~~)

It was as though the moths had been excised, the dusk after the first hay cut. Another exercise in the control of green, of the long sappy grass, of the wide wind sweep of slight susurrating as quiet as the sand-slow percolating of running-off water. Rilled by the rain, growth points a nick below the flailing blades, shoot up again, hard, sharp, itch, prickling with hoverings, heaving murmurings of dipteral things in the swept-low mown tide of slash-cut tips, all upstarting again, softærly winging it.

Naming of grass
(with thanks to Henry Reed's 'Naming of Parts' published on 8 August 1942 as a 'poem from the forces', regrown here on 8 April 2024 as a poem from the farm.)

To-day we have naming of grass. Yesterday it was long lines of greening. And tomorrow morning we shall have what to do after the clearing. But, today, we shall have naming of grass. John Deere's yellow and green high shine like mirrored glass in all the neighbouring fields. And to-day we have naming of grass.

This is the leaf sheath, the ligule and leaf blade. And this is the growth point at the base of the leaf blade, the importance of which you will see when setting the height of the cutter swing. And this is the second growth point at the base of the leaf sheath. Which in the field you will see, has not yet been reached.

This is the vegetative stage, which is always reached in tissues capable of growth from within the apical dome. Buds are sites for tillering. There are many terms that refer to buds. Terms like sprouts, shoots, daughters and tillers. There are aerial buds, adventitious and basal buds. But basically, all buds are buds. The buds are fragile. And please don't ever let those buds be broken, because broken buds cannot be awoken, and intercalary cells will cease to increase.

And this you can see is a rhizome. Some grass has this extravaginal tillering. This means they send out lateral underground growth which can node and turn into daughters. Grass species with extravaginal daughters are sod forming and can be invasive. This is underground growth here. And another undergrowth is stolon. Which we have (not) got.

They call it cutting the grass. It is perfectly easy; if you know how the grass grows, have chosen the right crop of haylage and the grass is wilted but not dry and the grass is chopped after cutting but before baling and if the bales are wrapped at least six to eight times in quality agricultural stretch black plastic before which always be sure to use Double Action Extra Strong additives. Which in our case we have. Almost silent back and forth the John Deere sickle bar scythes, and the fragile motionless hare humped proud like an unkicked clod, and above on the glide the buzzard scryes for sliced mice. We call this cutting the grass, scything rapidly backwards and forwards, assaulting and fumbling the Spring.

Wrung a warrening

(Mugwort, Plantain (waybread), Corn Salad (lombes cerse or stune), Nettle, Betony (adder-loather), Chamomile (mayweed), Crab apple (weregulu), Chervil and Fennel)

It was a shift sharp of a morning, and on the hallowing wind, *erce erce erce eorthan modor* wrung a warrening. In the straggle of remnant ancient, litter deeps and a forest gallows. In the flit-light slight of the gappy slits between leaves of the gall full oaks, swallows were arrow-fast winging the breck hollow of the once was coneys field wholly filled full of holes. This land planted, in the words of its planting and above, a jug full of blue. And all around, glory-twigs and wood-sour incantatory, and the white scut lollopings of inherited perspective.

From the frogbit, pleiades
(in milk moon reflections, from rain full ghost ponds, moths arising)

Restless, the meniscus. Shoals of *Cataclysta lemnata* rising milk white from spearwort much as seraphim dizzily spiralling at dusk to light. And between rafts of lily pads, floating fragment cases slow move on tremors, slight echoes through soft emerging Southern Hawkers clasped adrift on wax-like frogbit. Tiny white stars flitting spark-lit skim duckweed, pyralid wings eye spotted, ditrysian in duck egg blue.

Farmed out: a georgic for the depleting of seeds
(out of blood comes blood, all poppy populations to date have shown target site resistance to ALS-inhibitor herbicides)

For poppy control, suitably furrow a narrow width slowly. Plough at least a foot deep. Appropriately set skimmers ensuring post plough pressure is hard by and up close. Slice off topsoil. Upend it in the furrow. Avoid all green. Avoiding green means slugs leave. With no slugs, crows leave. When crows have left, there is control of surface disturbance and larks leave. When larks leave, you have control of the sky.

For poppy control, never allow germination. Seeds must deplete, must be buried sleep-deep. Not allowing germination avoids fertilisation and transient seed, and with no transient seed, there are no slight stems, no bled white sap when broken, no scarlet pockets of resistance littering edges with aggrieved corolla and silk slick damps of unpacked calyx cant in ditches, and no flushed crush of bled petal red.

For poppy control, use low raked angling of many winged tines. Go back and forth several times. Make seed horizons long, the longer the better but best in class is elementary, use the strongest spray chemistry for the avoidance in corn of the bled-red tell tales of what the war-sent and then absent farm hands all knew as the Suffolk canker rose.

Geometrical omissions
(on the limitations of seeders and sprayers)

In the Iron Age ring cycle dips, skylarks and a paucity of seeds.

In the boomsprayer's tramlines, weeds and the busyness of bees in steep decline.

Counting crows
(carrion crows can produce a deliberate number of vocalizations on cue, which is "a very impressive achievement", says neuroscientist Giorgio Vallortigara, Nature, May 2024)

Deliberately cawing, these rows of intoning crows count beats reliably and, much as Mozart's planned advance of auditory cues for a dance, are cognitively controlling chance. These wings tip a skip and a roll in a long slow jive. These *Corvus corone* have always known more about caw commands (and carrion) than ever a human can.

Strong chemicals, wet harvest

I remember standing; watching them fix giant Lacey Air Sweep grain-dryers, electric motors on cross-conveyors, and acres of flood lights on cantinas strung across empty grain barns – the size of aircraft hangers. Hollow and howling. Agcat crop sprayers lurching under High Tension Cables, the pilot waving. Tankers of pesticide. Smell of tin and fluorine. Aldrin, paraquat and DDT in drums down the lane, MCPA, mecoprop and dichlorprop. Cold cattle grates, straw walkers. 60Kilowatt fans and a rain of grain tumbling.

The formation of abscission layers

It may require forced separation or abscission of covering parts. It may require expansion of epidermal cells in the midrib. It may require the abscission of cover, horizontally, along the entire circumference. The cover may be soft, sepal-like tissue. Or more woody. Or there may be a vertical slit of a sepalous covering structure. Sometimes flowers never close, and petals abscise when the flower is still open. Sometimes petals drop.

Thin alluvium, we plough the field and scatter
(everything rises, designation of a district)

It is a resource block. It has (unequal) boundaries. It is a hundred-acre square of land of which eighty acres of thereabouts bores mineral. No account was taken. For example of ways, villages, land of high agricultural value nor of any landscape value. Nor of anything that might prevent future exploitation. In decades to come. No trees. No hedges. No account of value was taken. Borders will be crossed. It must be emphasized that the assessment is applied to the resource block as a whole. No parts will be interrogated. Only the hole. Holistically. Valid conclusions cannot be drawn from parts. Or from potential. Or from past participles. Or from compositional form. Or from soundings. Or from the way in which fields are made up of bodies. Upon bodies. Subcrops cropping up beneath Pleistocene. Shark's teeth, the remains of turtles, it was (is) a Tropical Sea. And in the clay, the drift and the coralline. It is a creamy morning. It was. The sandy limestone was (is) full of spiralling fossil shells. And the Stour was (is) meandering. And in the field, grain is growing in the uppermost geology. And in the grain, bodies were (are) underlain and phosphatised bones had (have) scrim in between. And the *here* and the *there* was (is) distillating. And in the migrating of bodies upwards and across the block, and in terms of overall form, here a Roman remains, here Saxon severalls, and here in the mourning the slow forming of fog between the upwelling and burying of bivalve and gastropod shells, coprolitic debris and teeth, layers upon layers of leaf and fallen sheaf and here metamorphic rock with lungfish traces, an ambergris squid beak in a paleo geographic eddying, and there in the seafloor-bedrock outcrop, fingerfuls of cobble silt and granulating bone bodies becoming the field that it is.

Corpse coins, becoming green
(a tarnishing, the grass reclaims remains)

It was a fracture of a dusk, split between the east and the west, the sky fricative and in the westwards racing fragility, crows.

Riding high swept black over tempered oaks and under hulls of yawing clouds low braced and ormolu in the over-risen river, wild-glass mirrored in the flooded common fennages, crows.

And in the in-breath instant of still, clay clods and short-horned cattle meadowing. Crow prone, we stay mud-laying mole dug up, face down, losing our lustre in the slow green devourings of oxidising rain. Above winging, beyond the limits of our vision, company-keeping, crows.

In between the in between

it was a mesenteric morning with red threads, a harslet of sorts, a disparagement of entrails spread, a slow coagulating of blood and fast bloating, umbels of a thin fallow unravelled, green bones broken like runic sticks, a slick of scavenging, fox watched, the heart-parts crow eaten. At the edge, under tall small-leaved limes, three fox cubs battling leaf slit sparkles in a shifting flicker of the fracturing light. In through the fissure slips the terror of the dawn.

The Geometrical Swelling of Yellow; the invention of the umbrella
(how to stay aligned whilst bending, and telling the time)

swellable the cortex, petal yellow the explodium, and in the fullness of blue, the noon day sun. Apical the plate, radial the patterning, and in the hygroscopic opening of feather-full pappi, the actuating capture of vascular fibre, floats. filamentous the ubiquitous dandelion, radiant with radical holding angles, anchoring resisting vasculature and in the swollen motion of the avoidance of dehiscence, in the sensing of the air, the cohesive co-ordination of the collective moment, the forward movement of a head of soft pappus hair towards a swell-full sprung-out metamorph on a sea of high humidity and, in a single synchronic motion, an opening umbrella aligns a hinged biology of bend, and sends to the sky perturbations of geometry and signals the tell tales of time

The drawing of words; sermons in (mill)stone
(sigils and summer plough days)

Fist of bees
ghost moths lekking
mackerel sky, blackening
breaking the back of the wheat,
the still,
the small (voice),
hearing the Miller's Word.
The bread-of-life, the incessant water
the thunder over the heat
pitter patter paternoster
for as long as it takes to say the Lord's prayer
or the Creed:
how many Hail Marys for sour dough to rise,
how many to get the toad bones out.

Spawning; the ghost in the field at dusk
(on resurrection, on sediment, on sticklebacks, and on being overtopped by trees)

Root-clung newts in a silt of fallenness watch water boatmen swerve and spider-like calculate a jump avoiding, just, a great drop from above, and in the weaving stem forest, a flickering picture fluctuating with a slight slipping breeze and then the typhoon of the Hawker's wings' tectonic flapping.

On the upper edge of tiny greens, roots and stems without end, drip-lines of frond topplings, and in the mirror moon reflections, a refraction of light, and from this rain full ghost-pond, eelpouts and sculpins ritualize sticklebacks and the ancientest of heliacals start sparkling arisings. Scales tipped, bullheads bristle pectoral in stony trickles pooling, part-shaded by the over-topping of trees, making their way to the Stour.

This dip in the land, horse-deep, a resurrection ecology wrought by the incessant Spring rains, a pre-historical remaking of ancestral DNA. In this unburial of mud, life.

New full dew pond

(the remaking of impermanent things when time is not about to stop, or conditionally upon the present, the future does not depend on the past)

In the pond, perfect circles and complications of water scorpions and hog-lice. The smooth newt's brood emerging in the unwrapping of forget-me-not-leaves watched by phantom craneflies and above, alder-flies' hatched larvae slow drop into the water, spreading tiny rippling rings under the low drone of furry bee-mimicking hoverflies. In the few-flowered spike rush, the grass snake eats a medieval medicinal leech watching a golden-eyed toad watching a whirligig beetle bubbling up mud. Clung with tiny trapezes of lepidoptera, emergent water soldiers solitary a three-petalled white flower arresting the patrol of the Palaeozoic Southern Hawker for just as long as the stopping of time or for an epiphany in the exercise of the use of rhyming language.

Unstable dispersions

It was the green; it was the press of that
and the warm smell of honeysuckle, it was that
and the breath and the blue of the jaded barley
it was turquoise green, it was shade, it was

                                          blue

blue green the barley grew, and it was that
it was the smell when the rain calms rock
and stone sends spores that spell petrichor
it was the moss and the breath it took, it was

                              intense with dew

it was this; it was where pollen grains land
and the passing of light and the fading of green
and the low sun hung and the landing of that
it was germination, it was seeds, and phthalo blue it was

                                  delphiniums.

Slant cubitus

A fletch, a call of fox, lambs ululating, a curve
a circle declined, a Crow moon
a fall, three stars aligned, Jupiter inclined
the Plough dissected; a nebula catched
stretched a finger, a nail, a bone, an ell, a bow, a cubital rest,
slant jointed, drawn aversus tip to wrist
hatched, prone, low strung & sloped
eln latched cubitus
leaning, bent of bow, unhinged,
forearmed & flung, the ulna of the owl.

In trinities, the building of permanent things when time is impermanent
(the counting of breaths and a cuckoos calling out its measuring of this road killed death)

    In between the pitter patter of the pater noster, a hailing of Marys, a creed and the dumb beat of Latin intonation, components shift and a disassembly of ribs (spread), hips and clavicle, a pelt soft red rust light-spiked with fracture-slant motes slow drifting, still and warm in the hovering sun, a hard glancing, pert black-tipped ears swivel perked to hear, thumb wide feather ended tail tight tucked right up and under part-sprung curled back legs, pads and claws hardly worn, pink tongue tip, tiny ivory incisor, a cub always, for ever and ever, just about to stop. ~~Again.~~

Holding on

It was a swift-shrill screaming sky of a morning, the grass feather-full and drifts of pollen rising. And under your wing, dark shadows, and a pronounced thoracic skew. And rising from the mist, the size of ocean liners, Belted Galloways puddling clay and in the smearing, you elaborate and dorsally hypertrophic are chasing the verticals in reaves of sweeping green, hawking from hoof prints rung a dislodging, ovipositing and in the kink-grazed cow-wheat, in a skimmer of heat, you hang a hover-cling and in a wing beat, define symmetry.

A catechism on supposition
(According to Suetonius, Isidore of Seville in the 7c says that verse is so called because the ancients used to write like they ploughed, i.e. back and forth)

Suppose the soil to be destitute, to be barren. Suppose what is drawn is not restored, suppose grass when the land is ploughed up. Suppose ploughing in green begets further green. Suppose turnips grow from bones alone. Suppose crushing and sifting. Suppose bone earth. Suppose bone dust and vitriolic dissolution. Suppose mixing with seed, a growth of new grass. Suppose grazing and re-grazing. Suppose burned bones and gelatine. Suppose the land supplied with that of which it was robbed. New grass sprung from earth of bones. Suppose night soil, ammoniacal, suppose the slaking of lime, suppose a light constant fleering of rain, suppose the composition of barley, and this flint full land well-draining. Suppose a healthy stock state to supply the daily waste of bones, of salts in the blood, suppose a fattening stock, suppose rich juicy grass and fibrous mashes, suppose water clear and sweet, suppose rotten rock and dead matter. And peripheral to a hundred acres of silent barley stood struck still, in the *sulh sulh* of the soil, I suppose the back and forth, the back and forth, the back and forth of the land.

Breaking bones, ~~on being aloof~~
(on the immutable relationship of forage quality and bone composition, and the changes experienced by dead matter)

Yes, I would keep my cow houses well ventilated, warm, dry and clean. And I would name them. I would feed my cows at regular

intervals, at least three times a day. And yes, when the vegetable matter has discharged its office in the animal bodies, it will return to

the earth in the form of dunging. And then, when entering the roots of new plants, which yes then will produce more newgrown offspring

with good high metabolization on rumination which then when the fertilized phosphatic pasture is foraged will increase the breaking

strength of the cannon bones of cows grazing, and yes *here a moo, there a moo, everywhere a moo-moo* making good strong bones for

later breaking.

Unhistorical acts
('Further [Achilles] set in the shield a soft ploughed field, rich tilth and wide, the third time he ploughed; and many ploughers therein drave their yokes to and fro as they wheeled about. Whensoever they came to the boundary of the field and turned, then would a man come to each and give into his hands a goblet of sweet wine, while others would be turning back along the furrows fain to reach the boundary of the deep tilth' The Iliad of Homer)

a tractor tyre backing over and over and over the brittle shells of larks and instead of sky, they become earth, and instead of song, unusual greenness and a dawn soiled, the sun bullfinch pink arising over just another soft ploughed field

Caterpillars' evolution
(variants of the offensive)

      Noticing
that farm tractors fitted with
caterpillar tracks rode ruts and
trenches as easily as paddle-
less ships at high sea, a yellow-
belly agri-cultural company
engineered endless steel
treads and this, the 'Greater
Application of Mechanical
Power to the Prosecution of an
Offensive on Land' (a pillering
worm way of moving) stemmed
the haemorrhage of starving
farm hands sent from the
Stour mud of Suffolk's *de rebus
rusticis* to Flanders's flooded
field drains, autumn rains and
insatiable mud becoming
ravaging rivers of rivets and
blood, stirred not shaken,
given not taken.

Suitable pins to pin your Heart Moth
(once plentiful at sugar in June, Dicycla oo)

You brindled beauty, you. No small fry, no fritillarying votaries, floating. No micro-lepidoptera meeting with me fleetingly in honeydew as does *Noctua, Bombyx* and other angels with brocade wings, but no not you, odd specimen, brindling

You, you on the wing, in the space between central shade and a submarginal line more or less suffused with dusky reddish grey, cinnamon and burnt umber, are dwindling

an intermediate form traversing a band of darker colour, your fore wings slightly dusty in fascia form ferruginous and the ground a kind of white or harvest yellow mineralling to ochre before termen in ash. Subdorsal slender, feeding on the foliage of Oak. Black above brown. Tagmata, more or less interrupted. Spiracling head, on a plate, tympanal, and on the first ring of your thorax glistening, stemmata black and shining, coruscating.

You your glory all departed, imago pinned a fringed wing, your dismembered heart your stigmata, you *Delenda est Carthago*.

A kind of wasp
(~~flight buzz~~, *a lamentation for the obsolescence of farmers*)

seeding via the spinning disc of agro spray drones, for the undersowing of standing crops. Sowing insecticidal biopesticides under cover of darkness, dropping fertilisers with low granular blends over hectares of wet summer land and, after agronomical calculation, an ode to slug pelleting. Independently an imitative formation swarms long distance, and then precision pre-armed threnodically with a deep odic hymn, swells in exultation and overseeding in the post-plough stave, puck drops the perfect pitch and from well beyond our visual line of sight reinvents with multi-rotor hands, the future of farm flight.

Unthankful villages
(farming not fighting)

The farmers came back, and the farm hands. A clapping gap between them. Before they went, it was all hands on the land, together to gather. So long as there was seed, there was harvest. After that the alivest thing in the field was peripheries and the ash of the bones.

The Golden Promise; embryo rescue and the multiplicities of many-rowed malting barleys
(X=7, agrobacterium-mediation, and non-brittle hexastichon spikelet fertility)

As if it were the action of the seed, as if it were the action of the sowers, as if it was the furrow or *sulcus* so named after the sun *sol* which naked mud sees when ground is ploughed out, broken after the fall, as if. As if it were the action of the plowers and the hard iron before the seed was cast abroad, as if it was the clear sky and the lack of rain, as if it were the cutting back, the farrago, as if it were the reaping, the blades, leaves and sheafs, as if it was the swelling tip, the *spiculum*, the beard so called because it is dries out first, the stalk *culmus* then the stem *calamus* followed by the husk, as if piss lit, as if it was six-rowed barley, quickly gathered. As if, as promised, it was *centesimus*. As if weighing the sun was enough.

The Seven Pillars of Pesticide

(acetamiprid, clothianidin, dinotefuran, imidacloprid, nitenpyram, thiacloprid, and thiamethoxam, or the revising of flight tables for hymenoptera)

That the frenulum connects the hind wing to the fore wing, that this hooking makes these two wings a single wing during flight, that this bristling leading edge fronts efficiency, that these apoidea drink nectar, honey and eat pollen and other than moths, maintain petiolic waists > that she fills her rose-leafed origami pots with honey and pollen for her young, that she reuses old beetle timber burrows, and calmed by scent, homes the homeless bee, that she provisions her nest with a single caterpillar on which an egg is laid, that dipterous prey is impaled upon her sting, that she is almost always solitary and hums lullabies where hundreds of blooms are born > that she succumbs to the exertions of neurotoxins irreversibly binding her nicotinic receptors, that she dies. That the flowers she burst into bloom die > that then, hum lulled we do too.

Adderbolts gaping
(the hitching up of wing buds)

then the dawn translucent emerges pupal wet in an exoskeleton of softærly eclosion, instars still visible, the moon mothed, the sky not yet hardened up, and below a moult, a chrysalidic exuvia skin split, a gape and a nymph-climb from water inspiring an exhalation, a wing expansion, dark tip marked, dehiscive, a germinal drying out, hitched up inchoate, a sprout, a bud, another slow sturr of the out-fall shitfull on an idyl of a riverine rural day

after-ripening

after auxin, pattern formation
a taproot sets in the garden
first a hypocotyl and two cotyledons
all folded over as the embryo grows
seed coated and mid-heartened

then turning green, torpedoes
oiled and waxed toward germination
either seedling lethality or apical lineage
dependent expression of allelic tissue
patterned and lodged in the meristem

the soil smells of damp Labrador and blood
the impress of me uprooting trees
old and cold remembering
heavy rain wintering ground with pellucidity
where hollow wings boned once keened
in an ash grey snow lightened sky, then with
elongation
root to shoot, canonises time transcribed radically
by RNA methylation

The (mis)timing of Summer
(constrained phenological plasticity)

It was early, the trees were going blue, old men's beards were filling the warm southerly breeze, stinging weeds were as tall as the trees and there were few bees, fewer wasps and seeds were past pollen releasing via sprinklings of grass grappling moths, and in the field maples were already on fire between toppling ragwort gold-cleaved with autumnal striped plunderers pillering. It was the harvest dust and the rain-filled phenological change, it was red turned black a month early, it was quiet angels lekking in the bird-light sky flickering through dry tipped peaks of indifferent grass, predator-less web-less, lepidopterous-less, a mis-matched dearth of tender taxa crashed in trophic level asynchronies.

Crowsticks; congregations with bells

('Every One shall do his best to destroy Crows etc… Every Town, Hamlet of more than ten dwellings …. provide and maintain Crow-nets during ten years. The inhabitants shall during ten years assemble and take order to destroy Crows, Rooks etc.')

That magic meant to scare rooks from crops, that flailing bundle of crowsticks dripping bad blood, that festering nested cant to kill ~~our feathered friends~~, that choughs and ravens be (de)spared. Wind-blown those crows barrelling over parallel rows of restless wheat, the gas guns blasting the hunting up of the rounds of steepled bells. The concentration to stay aloft, half-muffled, to stay in time, not to fluff the flow. Royal the number of bells, ten, loyal the number of crows peeling off to the east, as solemn in procession as the cacophony allows.

Food plants
(and Deilephila elpenor)

I am not a successful gardener and I can't farm; I can't harm a thing. Perennial nettles tower over me feeding caterpillars and releasing frilly Comma colonies, and there are more every year. The rhizomatous rooting rosebay willowherb that I saved from the flail repaid me with a hatched clutch of hawking pink elephants, for which their bubble-gum and brassy-green camouflage is an exact colour match.

Bringing in the green
(sun upping)

and

just when I was losing hope, I saw

two southern hawkers shape hearts mating high in the wildlife corridor we made, and

in the hedgerow cherry-plum we planted, wild honeysuckle, and

forty-three solitary bees in the wildflower meadow we sowed this spring, and

uncountable meadow browns gatekeeping in the keeling grasses we no longer mow, and

red kites circling where the molehills are amassing and rabbits are brecking the land, and

a charm of goldfinches strong-tugging thistle fluff because we no longer flail, and

in the ragwort, a colony of cinnabar caterpillars feeding, and

on an inside edge of an old horse shelter we saved two pupating emperor moths tight silk wrapped & waiting, and

in the jumbling brambles we don't scythe, a spiral of peacocks scattering amongst the pink edged flowers, jostling with admirals on slumping damsons sticky-gnawed by drunken wasps, and

underneath, fox scat filled with stones and pelt and bird-cherry pits, and in the towering umbelliferous wild carrot, crepitation and a massing of humbug hover flies, and

beneath the brassicas leaves we grow, little adherings of butter yellow eggs and an insisting line of black ants farming bunches of greenflies and carrying off in circuitous trailings of wet sweet scarlet, our over ripening drip squish of this late season bumper of strawberries, and

next to the old English hedge we plashed, a hedge sparrow watching, on piled brush-cuttings a blinking lizard watching us counting stag beetles in the rotting tree-limb colonnade we only recently made, and

under a leaning sheet of corrugated tin, a grass-snake and curling nest of neonates stirring our decomposing mountain of beetle-busy composting, and

in the jay-blue sky, keening of buzzards calling on the thermals circling with the canting jackdaws high hurtling, and

skating on the pond we dug from the old San's boiler-house clinkered ash and sand, waxy whirligig beetles dizzily eating expiring china-mark moths wings vacuum-pinned to the quivering meniscus, and

clung to bullrush stems, water snails and dry exuvae splitting to reveal soft new nub-winged southern hawkers, and

in the gall full oak, a fledgling tawny owl perching buddha-like and wide-eyed sees its very first dawn, the sun low and slow to arrive, and

sky me high dragonfly, in the addition of it all, *dulci jubilo*, a celestial shower and megastrobilus, with meiotic division, misrule – and I catch a fall of ovuliferous angels, a plash of cones, blood berries and a hart wassailing coloraturas, chewing cud and eschewing scat cunning and

gloria in excelsis

Heritage
(a denial of divinity)

In the dark of the green, towerings and trees going blue, and in between the early bats, oak lands and stumps of a tangible light, tangles of brambles and fallings as prone as backbones of longhorn cattle at dawn, germinal and gold. Tail feathers on the ground, half a horse shoe, mouse remains, a brachiopod sea risen, a musket ball, a crow bone, red coralline crag. In the hush, too much history. Under the shawm stalk, this land is our own unowned deepest past.

Hunting ♯
(hung dead, swung chimed, – during the Magnificat, the bell is struck 9 times)

Three re-hung, tuned C *sharp* and two in B and monophonic in the oak and after firing, squirrels swung and dying and along the stave the chain toll of yesterday wrung out of living and interrupted swapped pelts over lapped in successive blows, an echo hunting up the slow decay. In the adjacent harmonic of whirred and beaten trees, rooks rise simplified wings a clapper, ringing the rung of change, and in the hum, tierce, quint and nominal all cant above the prime and at the strike, as a pebble in a pond, see sound arisen with the forbidden crows pealing east wherein laid down is plain direction for pricking and discovery of misterie, bounties and firing up instructions for hanging *lugeo mortuos* and other immaterialities for all swung rotationally slow dangling by the leaping rope hunting up and hunting down chime leading the taut array, much as hounds holler a clamour out of time, cast ringing a shattered toller of a wild-goose chase across this mute field of the dead belling of Stedman sound.

Belief in evergreens
(salvage)

                        dis-spoked contraptions of tractor-towed raking tines sink with rusting blood brown radial harrows, and weed-bound gaskets sump dump and drop metal prongs which drill disarticulated chassis lain prone growing sun with flowers, and in the combine harvester's cutting dust skeletal artichokes sharp poke vertical and intricate the sky, heart and keel, towering over. Lightly the tread, bones resistant and rusted wait, and limb-squint in a rake of haylage, a number plate from 1968

The underside of leaves
(or Early Warning Systems)

    It was stefenic, a mouth, a bone
    as one sea into another, an opening
    alone

    it was a marker, on the underside of leaves
    a union, an intersection, a communion
    between

    it was a scattering of holes, the site of polyphenols
    an aperture response to losing vapour, it was
    closing

    it was the place of climate change, of gaseous exchange
    terrestrial flux and transpiration, leaf
    along water loss inducing stomatal stress,
    it was patterning parenchyma reducing guard cell turgor, it was
    clustering

    and stained brown in mouse eared
    Arabidopsis thaliana L., it was
    extruding

    tiny mouth marks on the underside of leaves

    and meristemoid, it was

    four lips twittering in the mine.

Farm accounting
(2 fishers, 3 urchins and 16 sparrows)

First it was the tipping out of hollow bones, then the planting of vertebrae in the 'old dispensation', my fingers in the prodding holes and I can smell the cutting, and in the settling dust no gain, no gleanings. Above a hundred acres cleared, I can see the rooks circling remembering bounties paid for a few ears of grain, and the loppings off of childrens' hands and the hangings by the neck, and the missing loaves risen again sprouting in the rain. And the fishes mud sturred, beasts puddling the cud, and I can count the corn and the horn in the high of the heat, stink spraddling between common and accounting values, between the unledgered living and the double-entried dead.

On coming to a standstill
(the waning and the drying up)

Having come to a standstill, the bare fields are open wide, all chewed out post barley harvest, pre the ploughed in stubble. The soil desiccated, the combine satiated, the measure of the ground, the grain, the gain, the grind, the small beer, the measure of the law, the land, the short-lived calm, the gizzards, the masticated black punk rot, the fungivorous spong, the remains of the drawn and quartered soil that dead-levelled will reclaim us all.

Church accounting – Blessed are the Birds psalm 84:3
(unholy archaeology, numbering bones)

❡ Edward Owles' bill for glazing done at the church, Oct 1828. ❡ George Mallett's bill for beer, rum, tea, biscuits, etc., Jun and Jul 1827. ❡ Appointment of Robert Grier, clerk, as curate of Huntingfield with Cookley, 9 Jul 1828. ❡ J Cooper's bill for (beheaded) sparrows, Apr 1828. ❡ William Cox›s bill for beer for ringers, at Christmas and for parish business, Nov and Mar (?). ❡ Isaac Mudd's bill for work done at the church, Aug and Nov 1827. ❡ S Norman's bill for repairing surplices. ❡ J Cooper's bill for (beheading) sparrows, 1828. ❡ John Mower's bill (as sexton), undated. ❡ Receipt for quit rent, manor of Huntingfield Rectory, for town land, 1 Jun 1829. ❡ William Rodwell's bill for work done at the church, Sep and Oct 1828. ❡ Receipt for quit rent, manor of Peasenhall, Huntingfield feoffees, Michaelmas, 1828. ❡ Similar, manor, Michaelmas, 1828. ❡ Receipt for land tax, Huntingfield feoffees, 18 Apr 1829. ❡ Receipt for quit rent, for 3 dosin of sparrow heads. ❡Paid for 5 Dussin of Sparrows heads ❡ Paid for 2 Dussin of Sparrows heads. ❡ January the 17th day out for the beheading of birds, a total sum of 6d. Hail Mary❡

Still, Life
(stopped time is a place)

>Dropped damson,
>the quick of the trouble,
>the crack of a twig,
>a slipped lizard,
>the disappeared.

>Having honed our knives,
>our scythes, bright
>like the fox, slunk of vixen
>scent, bunt struck,
>co-axial, farmed out.

>Those arrangements
>of leaves on stems,
>the georgic
>that gives
>the pastoral
>its rank, shrunk,
>stopped
>identity, the *Et in Arcadia Ego*
>husbandry of our time.

Earth-movers

(earthing up — where soil goes, souls follow)

That this dust, this sand, this soile, this post-harvest craquelure, this fracture, this dry, this hard place, this autochthon sprung from, this descent from self, this fundus, sole of the foot, this mud, this miry earth, this lupin choking out of the weeds, this feeding of the ground, this dirt grown and hog wallow, this rotten, this archaic bog-night, this farmed-out bottom of the hearth, this flay flint, this shingled grit, this depletion, this erosion, this uncommon, this disembodied aureate, this is ground, hallowed out, this soil hollowed is followed by our souls.

For the unadulterated lex loci or the tout ensemble
(with thanks to Dr E. J. Russell's Lessons on Soil, 1911)

If used Passively & Substituted for activity It fails. Like snails after scattered glass.

Local phenomena must be dealt with as the weather permits Opportunities may pass And never return A loss irreversible A curse or worse

Loose in almost any lane, field, stream or hill, the material is practically Complete. Use feet. Stand.

Pot experiments should be started. Twenty flowerpots are wanted for the set being the same size, about 8 inches being convenient, they must be kept warm, and never wet

Three are to be filled With sand and swarm Seven with subsoil & the remaining ten filled again with good surface soil No till, no tilth, no tide, no roar   no recoil

Three of the subsoil pots are uncropped Two being stored Moist and one dry by and by Four pots of surface soil are cropped And moist A fifth and sixth are crocks And old stick bone dry One of these contains earthworms, red And thin And moist, not dry, coiled, not dead

Four glazed pots are also wanted Be they jam or marmalade jars desired besides Mustard Buckwheat Rye Make good crops Leguminous crops however show Certain abnormal characters and do not grow Turnips and cabbages are apt And certainly, to almost fail Avoid snails, glass gutted entrails entailed trails and undesirable lines

None of these should be used It is highly desirable that the pots should be Duplicated complicated fragmented composted Abscised layered & earth worms are very useful a Coalition of Willing Almost anything that can be Consumed by fire can be consumed by, turn   bend, don't burn worms.

Others are abject And sheep occasionally Limp and may occasionally die staring at the sky

Worm cast patch the heft and lear. As far as possible KEEP OFF   the heaf   The clay and stay With sand or chalk

Walk Don't run don't try to catch the sun If a stream or hill are accessible The material Is practically complete or Plots two yards & square will suffice And a steady supply of sand And clay obtained any way If the soil is burnt it is never the same despite the rain

Clay is exceedingly useful dig some up To make land take mud add sheep on the heaf Add experiments with sand Lime makes clay less sticky It should be kept in a well corked bottle Add worms They are very useful Examine a piece of dry   Land should never be buried but always carefully be kept on top Put up soil in early July sow at the end of September Add sky Pour rain   Mud is relief   particles stick together The soil is full of living things   They drag in leaves, Magpie feathers and sealing wax. What might happen if they would not.

Announcement of domain, counting tweets
(the cantata, a wind ensemble, the entire hollow, fugal counterfeit)

calls a disyllabic *hueet*, or a soft *huitt*, chiff chaffling supercilium in caesura, grubby white in underparts descending a projection, tinkling a paraphrase wide spreading with added drum, a monosyllabic duet, a piping pew, a slight blue hued *Carpinus betulus*, a subdued diagnostic commonly in pairs, occurring in the autumnal glare, in buffish-brown, irruptive *kip kip kip* delivered in flight, rattling primarily on seeds of alder and of birches, thin twigs and black bibs wheezing *chek-chek-chek* trill twanging a *tveeht* prominent with archangels trademark pollen gold wingbars yellow in low light, radiant and bird-sized

Und leuchtet wie die Sonne / Matris in gremio. / Alpha es et O. /
(lethal coloratura, the downed flight feathers of birds)

        faith full to areas of good feeding, song seldom heard in the region, beech proliferates rocking, flocking on an F sharp breeze uttering invertebrate declining an agile siren, and in the dead of night a trill, a habitat of deep and coppiced cover with macaronic mud-lined leaps much like October's florid orange flanks makes lethal irresistible and subsequent call identification easy

Tax Collection
(the annuntiatus)

Dearly Beloved, do not think that because scritch by scratch the wasp chews the widening patch of hard wood soft as pollen dust, do not think that because the gyrinidae beetle waters with whirls raking soft ellipticals, do not think that because the share, coulter and hake gave this place it's shape, that the farmlands at this eleventh hour hold still their form, that before the rain comes the cows will face the wind, the sows will wild rootle the straw, the horses will stamp unsettle, the crows as one will rise and search for higher skies, do not think to take the ashes of wormwood, sage, lavender or that because the wheat, orient, is slaked with heat and everything umbilical simmers with the quick of it, and the crotch bone floats wishing downstream against the grain, do not think that this apparatus of perturbation, this unsyncopated relation of ecological stock is gingerbread, is helletropium. On the contrary Best Beloved, as fast as the shell on an egg *teste me ipso* this future will be our ~~past~~ last.

A divinity of bees, deceased
(a georgic of sorts, never grow lemon balm on a farm)

Needed reagents are lysis buffer, acid phenol, chloroform, isopropyl alcohol, ethanol and sterile RNAese free water. And 200 bees from a field colony. Or 30 to 50 from a cage experiment. Count them into centrifuge tubes. Flash freeze and autoclave. Collect 50 bees from the tube, place in a resealable sample extraction bag. Add buffer. Remove air. Seal bag. Smash with rolling pin until all the bees are broken, being as helpless as a babe in a Cretan cave.

Xylogenesis; an (Edenic) gap
('strokes of havoc unselve' Gerald Manley-Hopkins 'Binsey Poplars' felled 1879)

Hewn, felled, be-felled, all fallen in, eyes sawn through, stalled and stolen. Elysian fields in one fell swoop struck-cut, snare trapped and sudden gone to ground, brought to earth, a de-throning as misplaced as lichen corridored in cork-lined drawers desiccating in Highly Polished Places. Dendritic the dawn sky, drawn down along the horizontal tree, morphological architecture de-barked, rossed and lignin split, consequentially a hacking off of tensile strength and root strain, the modulus of elasticity and cambial logged time, severing the anchorage of history of when dew, after xylem rising, began its inevitable fall.

High Site Fidelity
(mercury stable isotopes found in Dragonfly larvae)

You, mercurial you, bioaccumulate. You, wet depositing, lentic and lotic, you bio-sentinel tell us the unstable places of the hidden traces of atmospheric mercury. Your efficacy, your ubiquity, your narrow trophic range, your high site fidelity, your larval tissue signals isotopic precipitation, your larvae bearing the biological burden of methylation, of heavy metals sequestration, you biomarking and vast tracking the vagrant trends of your larval pathway, making your iridescent way towards our global detoxification ends.

The pastoral side
(earth and turfed, debatably appointed)

This ditched coalition of compromise, ancienting hedge, bee anointed, espistling with thistles recovered in tiny flowers, a respite from stranglings of nylon baling twine, plastic tat and crisp crumpled Walkers packets from 1973. English as edges, read for roots, heaving towards meaning, snagging diction, dialectically medieval in its way, its own impetus and structure, ragged out with age, its presence an existence and exercise in dateable layering, bones of fallow deer, crab apple leaves skeletonised, galls of mite and the disinclination of hazels to mingle, to tangle with barbed wire, its rows never quite leaving the field, still shepherding.

Occurrences in fields
(sheep-walking the land of the barley barons)

From the air, the Romans are still there, and underneath the Saxons surfacing in places are breaking through for the metal detectorists, and in the great field the farming goes on and on, so long is the lay of the land, and champion the fields of sugar beet, the clearances, and in the shackage of the barley stubble, ewes fould-coursing for just as long as the midday tolls are heard twice belling but never for a single moment longer.

A distraction of congregations; on the wall porphyry is red
(end of the season p/reparations, feeding the birds)

This unreliable, this spidering into autumnal flare, this wordclept glare, these dangerous extra-ordinaries, this heraldic ferruginous green and clotted ochre red, this dragon flight and porphyric warmth, these decrepitations, these gales and cob-webbed vair, this cast pale sun, this beheading and kneeling, this bird-adorned faint Saint in tourmaline plaster peeling, ~~that damp illegibility, that spun lime-washed miracle of the cup (and slip), of adoration, of shepherds, two scenes not fully identifiable,~~ this echelon of geese, this gathering of leavings, this last ewe, this early fall.

Simultaneous; black henbane, the eroding edge of empire
(the barley fields of this one horse land)

Such is the continuity of fields used for the growing of barley that it is possible, seized in the present, to extend time at first glance backwards and then to permanence and other future vagaries, reaved and barely visible, except for centuries of weed seeds germinating under the barley prevailing whilst time passing thriving in these gravel soils laid thin edge-on-edge and end-to-end aligned against the wind. Arranged, these average ancient scaldy flint-pocked fields orientate north-west / south-east coaxialling, a little irregularly Celtic or Iron or Bronze or other unbounded stoney age save for the shadow of a hedge and the drop of a ditch and a rolling angelic way until then – when the Romans came right up and over the eroding empire edge bringing *contubernia* and black henbane hidden in hollow goat bones. That this presence, like flies in the autumn flare, unearths the present and unsettles plough-less horses is some   space   simultaneous   that has never not been there.

Domestication
(to be pulled from the earth)

We begin with myths and meteor glow and thereby and whereinbeforeafters. In words we become other things, things that walk on water, things that drown. We believe in archaeology, in the distance between bodies, in the inescapability of borders. In the fields, barley and oats are broken down and recreated to be incapable grain dispersing mechanisms with readily detachable ((bracts)) for the prevention of safe seed burial.

Being the shepherd;
having hard hooves and easy lambing traits
(first obtain your County Parish Holding Number CPH from the Rural Payments Agency RPA)

As close as new religion and derelict gods, the dunging machines ear-tagged and Roman nosed sense the direction from which the rain is coming, and like ancient deities in various states of decay, once lambed now eschewing myth-making, are puddled together under payne's grey making measured muck calibrated by the square foot, and drone surveyed. Between them, a hundred saints and hornless blue-faced holy lambs bleating and shitting deductions in strong chemistry and other subsidies necessary to become a fine boned bred-off-the-grass prolific sheep reaper.

The maples are in full flame, hedges flaring
(the rooks were scouring the pot)

It's mid-September. There are fresh green leaves on the walnut trees, red Admirals spiralling in mating curls, scarlet dragonflies in squadrons high firing and the french beans' flowers are agog with heavy bumblebees. Hard quinces are starting to gold, the plums are long gone and the fox has made a hideaway in the tipsy damson tree, pits and scat her giveaway. This, this is all wrong. Out of season, out of time. The wrong song.

Gall, or on never eating blackberries after Michaelmas Day
(being hedged-about and herbaceous)

Before the Romans came, battling aberrant archangels tipped the devil from hell from where he fell rampant and bottom up into autumn's hard-clawed thorns and hoary underneaths, and so cursing brambles spat spit on a rash of bitter pricks and on the marble-small balls of declining berries' reflexing calyx and the looped tight-clung close-clasped clonally trailing spent laterals colonised intractably by *botryotinia fuckeliana*, parasites and wasp pierced galls full of the last past, which scaldheaded were hedged-about much as was the old sprung-from rune and the subsequently-(un)saintly octobered Michaelmas Day.

Ordinary; left over from butchery
(with one visible eye)

                        les animaux de la forêt Net Weight two pounds, Cartwheels shiny and round, dead weight several Tonnes inanimate treadle-less threadless, red blue and stained Bones completely unbound, internal angles of zero u-n---s--t-i t--c-h---e--d and found four holed pin-shanked fish eyed and de-Horned mathematically re-formed in hOles

Intonation of generations of cattle-droving two centuries ago
(seeking seeds of small leaved limes)

Meeting tangentially at soft points, sheer heft of the living adhering and begin by knowing tessellation with no gaps as from the inside of onions soft skinning to the slight soft cells of mollusc shells & cusp like corners and deformed on the plane slicing this specific time and place shifting mining multitudes abundantly as wild service seedlings moving in from the edges scribbling & starkly in the thin of it. Think of it as resonance, the frequency of the strung thrum of the ground from where it is grown, thistling in the original act of writing itself down.

A de-composition
(being bioactive)

This is a lived experience. What kind of home is this? Tracks of hedgehogs, ducks, geese becoming a different sort of habitat, breathing from second to second, as standing in for the herbivores, I trim the grass seeking seeds of neglected trees and echoes of Jurassic feet.

And with the rooks you see river, you see sky, you see the horizon along which crows fly and underneath the flow you know there is a very different landscape, you smell soft white rot, propagules, you see the sexton and the burying beetles, you see the quiver of a spent feather and its descent on the breeze, you smell fire. And in the deadwood there is so much life, and in the ash you see the bone. What kind of biome is this? Elytra with raised longitudinal lines, abdominal tergits in gold, and fine hind tibia. And undertaking, dull not shining, pronotum wide and evenly rounded, and close up and low down, you are seeing the earth recycle.

I'm never going to get the sound out of my ears of my own neck being broken, my rib cage being crushed, my heart beaten. Under the hawthorn I reside, car struck there where I died. It was autumn and the sky was hard with salt and ice, and there was rime circling the hibernal night of a sanguine moon. I, astride the verge, am disintegrating, leaf seeping and dissolving. Silver slicing aslant my dehiscing, I was asunder the moon, and then with the slow spreading certitude of my split spilt pelt I fell under the thrall of the sweet neatening of the approach of the burying beetles.

Here below, there is no green at all. Shadow ditch and deadwood dived, fog basking in the autumnal dawn, these elytra caught micro-marbles of droplets slight shiver, stilling a tremble and on a slight slant stop just upended on the cusp of a slow fall to feed. I have no need for speed, being a darkling beetle, tenebrous and out to meet the polyvores.

Fungivoric *rubescens* blushing-bracket bruised pinkly red I spore-decay deadwood and sapwood just the same, and with a slightly bitter taste, gill-like I fan out lacking legs or a stalk having self-choreographed myself genetically with my bacterial friends from the sea to the land. Thick walled and much branched, with clamped and binding hyphae, I am popular amongst fungus-loving beetles and if you see my fruiting bodies, then as lignin-life my host is dead but the soil below is very much alive.

Seeing Blue

(how to stop the loss of water from wheat ears)

Erratic the rainfall patterns, at leaf level, mole flux of oats, of wheat ears, of pore aperture, of opening under spectral blue light and of guard cells gatekeeping the continuum between. Threads of thin water rise high and heaven sending to evaporate through a million stomata underneath each single leaf, a stomatal conductance in the removal of blue genes, and a driving of water use efficiency for the higher yielding of greens.

Bi O p (t) ics

(a moving picture)

Still.   Silent.   Cut out of the sky.   Spare   shaped. Pigeons hunch   feather full of air.   The bare walnut emptied of leaves, clotting with perching and   the   slow   creep   of   old ochre and the fog   full moss is deep. It was a meandrous morning; slight frilled   mint lichen was   misplaced and the mOOn still hung over   from the night before.   The grass verglas glazed   rigid. The sky, coagulating.   The   tall dried teasels   spindle toppling silverly and witheringly   ˙sharp hooked with whirls, are goldfinch flocked.   And filched of slight slivers. Greenly the moss   thaws and oaks island   this first autumnal frost and parch. Under   beeched leaves, driplines   and   wet   depths, mouse holds   and shivers,   the   blet scent   of hyphae riven sod and   of   dog-arsed medlars, vixen   scat, and the brown honey going over   sweet   aroma of quince quailing under the glaucous and round rolling ~~~ O-O-O-O-O-O-O- OO ~~~~~   thin tin white of the hunter's   mOOn   as   long-shadowed and greyblue   veined, it oculates.   Still the silence.   Spore-falls of mycelium arise and slow thread   the dead   wood, rot bedecked and with   mass-branchings   anastomosing hyaline slandering root strandlings   grow. I fancy   that I feel   in the   fey frost   struck   dawn   that   I   hear the   slow-fast colonisation beneath   my slow-fast freezing feet   of biota, of   propagules, of inoculum,   of wax caps, of   five   giant white   puffball   O O O O O   exactly   the   same size   as   the   m OO n

Field

(playing the)

Wet woods. Imbroglio. Where sky is trapped and there are no doors. Where water flows down so fast, conkers, seeds and sodden leaves, leave. And having left, cleave glass-green grass and sag. Verdaccio. Nothing but trees. Linden limes, five in a row leaves beginning to glow, goldening stems brown turning tourmaline. Dogwood high shines raw blood red. Wild cherry, willow wet beyond weeping bowing to the ground. Dead black walnut, leaf bereft, adorned with the heft of five wood pigeons and a young sparrowhawk yellowing. In the middle distance, young oaks, monopodial tips, a slew of jackdaws, no fences, no walls, incessant rain sounding down, hissing and spitting through the sky scraping pines. And the poplars silver side up are smoking green. This wood has no doors. Where sky flows, trees go. And remain. And seed and spread. With heads like caterpillared cabbages, shedding and smelling of intaglio.

Collective motion, or winter grazing of a fresh field of vetch
(a force field)

Idiosyncratic sheep particulate excitedly towards the goings over of fresh vetch and rye. It takes just one to go, like a photon emitted from (say) an atom, also excitedly. After the transitioning one, the flock follow on to the new green field and find themselves compelling a small attractive force field and thus aligning themselves collectively at the same speed in the same direction matching as attractively as idiosyncratically transitioned photons emitted from a particulately excited ram lamb atom.

Hockets

(æfen-sang around about the sixth canonical hour in the direction in which the sun sets)

The air was cold, the clouds low, pigeon pink and edged with charcoal. A ragged echelon of geese weft overhead wobbling in the key of C and there there above the fret of the oak and the filigree flicker of peeling birch, in the glowering fire of a sliver of sky just there a slight whisper across the valley of the vesper call of bells. And then amidst the back and forth of the tawny owls, the vixen's yip yip yowl and after the ringing sharp bark of the fallow deer, the twig crack and brittle-hustle of beech leaves underfoot, in that sudden silence of a quiver of clearing, in the taught pull sprung of the green new moon, in a summoning of the night Fin begins to howl.

Ancestries
(With some, it is like they never left, like they'd never gone. Like they belong.)

Standing for itself, that last ox-eye daisy. Nature morte this late in December, yet Et in Arcadia Ego; the crucible antecedent. The forms coming into being articulating yellow with extreme precision amidst the going over of green, of the edge browning of wild sorrel before turning to procedures for underground, pre-verbal. In the etymology of aftermath, rafts of spiders webs spread tensile shroud-thread catching all hoverings and lipid carapaces. The mole Homerically heaving up citadels is percolating down to Persephone amidst broken glass, sand and debitage. And underfoot millennia, archived in acres of ancienting, still enceinte with seed.

Raven
(a robotic avian vehicle for multiple environments)

This is the harvesting of the aftermath, this grey drone with bird legs and carbon fibre fixed wings. Versatile drumsticks, think chicken, think walk, hop and jump (joyless) into the air. Verily evocative of the real thing. This is a commotion of locomotion; autonomous take-off and multi-modal gait. This robot drone has bird legs, but lacking in all tradition, it can't lay eggs.

Coming back to land
(the power of regenerative tales)

In the delicate proximities
of brittle roots and stems, soil
siccative edges simultaneous
hermaphrodites secreting cocoons
for the enclosing of eggs, and – in the
turning over and over
and over again
of soil,
all-seeing Oligochaetes
hoping for rain, aerate
invisible indivisibles sending
souls back home
to regrow all over again

Weeping Hill; to be exactly placed, disinheriting perspectives
(I took a walk last century amidst all those ancient certainties)

a fraction indefinable on the head land, a stopping of the clock, a halt to the harrowing, a sky larking, a remnant woodland rook full. Stalk stubble grass crow-buried, an unbroken tract valley slant, a slight, a fracturing. Liking to follow the making of being, hedged about, those enclosed hallowed roads foreclosing fields, ceaseless water, another scant sun, snow melt and I stood hard by palimpsest disinheriting the perspective. Going over the headland, I knew the river flowing below, but I did not want to know its name.

Notes

The second quote under the epigraph page headed 'A (Modern) Pastoral' is from a translation by Kimberley Johnson of Virgil's *Georgics*, Book 1 (Penguin, 2009).

In the season of sowing barley; the vocabulary in this poem is still used, and is local to East Anglia being specific to the nature of this place. The words 'chamblings', 'chicked'. 'bossoching', 'clagged' 'freshes' and 'brauches' are georgic in and of themselves. For example, gardeners locally still chick their seed potatoes as they have for centuries. These local words have deep tap roots and are seeded in the fields.

Dip-tailed ouzeling; 'hagaþorn' is an Old English word for hawthorn, still sometimes heard here. It is a childhood word for me. Haga is haw (as in hips and haws) and the Old English letter 'þ' is also known as the 'thorn' thus enacting in its form, the nature of the thorny haw-filled hedge plant. I have always named it thus. 'Rattock' is a farming word, an old East Anglian term for making a lot of noise. Another childhood word.

Feeding on flowers; 'perresil' is the Old French word for parsley. It is also a phonetic rendition of how the word sounds locally, in dialect. It is the sound of locality, here.

Farming the last year; the word 'tenurial' is a crucible. It is an Old Anglo-French Latinate word holding multiple meanings in this poem. The title is an old farming saying, you can only ever farm the last (previous) year.

Mythology can ask; the subtitle is a paraphrasing by James F.W. Johns-ton in the introduction to his *Catechism of agricultural chemistry and geology* Edinburgh 1844, of Jonathon Swift in *Gulliver's Travels*.

Stigma; *Affodilus* is medieval Latin for daffodil. *Affodil* is also local to East Anglia. Daffodil has an amazing etymology which Geoffrey Grigson picks up on in his 1950s herbal. He says (p.416) "*Narcissus pseudonarcissus* owes a debt also to its English name, which goes back, through the Medieval Latin *affodilus* and Latin *asphodilus*, to the Greek *asphodelus*, name of that plant which grew across the meadows of the underworld and which belonged to Persephone, the Queen of Hell." There is an ancient tradition of forging nails on Good Friday, each hammer blow is a ritual of symbolism reflecting the act of crucifixion."

I felt a funeral in my brain; in a dominating style, he was painted; the first phrase of the title is from Emily Dickinson's poem of the same title. The under-titling words are taken from the Chronicle of Henry de Blaneford of St Albans Abbey in 1405, also in the *Guide Book to St Mary's Church, Wissington*.

Futhorc; the phrase '*And here I here the fowlis synge*', is taken from the medieval poem 'The Medieval Farming Year'.

All our hills were tangled wood; *each man dwelling in the midst of his own occupying*', as William Harrison put it in 1577).

The Red Massey Ferguson stands in for WCW's red wheelbarrow and whilst there are no longer white chickens here, there are ideas, a glaze of rain, in this land.

Unless you run your Head into a Hedge, you cannot but see them as you walk – Culpepper's comment on the pervasiveness of buttercups.

Loomweight; incorporates found text from *A breviary of Suffolk or a plaine and familier description of the country, the fruits, the buildings, the people and inhabitants...* Robert Reyce, 1638. Published 1902 by J Murray of London.

Canker rose: a georgic for the depleting of seeds; 'aggrieved corolla' is a phrase from John Ruskin's 1882 botanical memoir, *Proserpina; A Study of Wayside Flowers*.

Thin alluvium, becoming field, or Everything Rises; the phrase 'fallen sheaf' means a dropped and scattered quiver full of arrows.

The Geometrical Swelling of Yellow; the umbrella as biological hinge; I came across an open access research paper in 'Nature Communications' online at *https://doi.org/10.1038/s41467- 022-30245-3* which investigated and discovered that the dandelion is more of an umbrella than a clock and that the way in which it releases its seeds presents a promising biomimetic potential in robotics and functional material, *"Unlike other hygroscopic plant movements, the dandelion makes use of radially symmetric swelling to generate torque, which may help to synchronise movement of the roughly 100 hairs that are organised in a disk like geometry."*

Stopping time *(the remaking of impermanent things when time is not about to stop).* The title refers to the Stopping Time rule – which is a mathematical mechanism for deciding whether to continue or stop a process on the basis of the present position and past events. It is said that this rule will almost always lead to a decision to stop at some finite point in time. It is not an event. It is a random variable

Unthankful villages *(farming not fighting).* The title is referring, in the context of it being this year (2014) 100 years since the First World War, to the term 'Thankful Villages' given to villages to which all those who went to war, returned. Of 16,000 villages in England (iro), 41 are said to be so called. These villages have no war memorials, for they had no dead hands. With thanks to the ongoing research of Norman Thorpe and Tom Morgan www.historic-uk.com.

The gaping of Adderbolts; 'adderbolt' is the early name for a dragonfly, being adder (venomous snake) and bolt (arrow).

The bones of things are numbers *(church accounting).* Special thanks are due to Jean Deathridge, Research Assistant at the Suffolk County Archive for her painstaking efforts in tracking down records for me, and for her encouragement of my research into the centuries long treatment of our feathered friends as vermin and the payment for their bones in bounties from the church's tithings. The irony of beatification of St Francis and his veneration in medieval wall paintings on the walls of St Mary's in Nayland by Wissington whilst the law of the land between circa 1532 and 1850 required the extermination of birds is parodical. Sparrows (actual and biblical) numbers are in freefall in 2024.

A divinity of bees *(never grow lemon balm on a farm)*. The reference to a babe in a Cretan cave arises from Virgil's *Georgics*, Book IV (on bee-keeping) wherein the king of heaven (or Zeus as a babe) was hidden in a Cretan cave and fed by a unity of bees (souls – bees were thought to be the carriers of souls). Virgil is saying how much more is achieved when everyone pulls together, and is suggesting perhaps that this is how the republic should be organised. Lemon balm (*Melissa officinalis*) should not be grown on farms because bees will not leave their hives where it is grown and hence will not perform willing services of pollination for crops. This is because Melissa, the bee priestess, is the only one who may 'tell the bees' to do so.

Xylogenesis; an (Edenic) gap *(strokes of havoc unselve)*. The italicised sub-title is taken from Gerald Manley Hopkins' poem "Binsey Poplars" (felled 1879).

High Site Fidelity *(mercury stable isotopes found in Dragonfly larvae)* source *Environ. Sci. Technol 2024, 58, 13444-13455.*

Simultaneous; black henbane, the edge of empire *(the barley fields of this one horse land)* It was rurally known that heavy clay is three horse land, that middling loam is two horse land and thin sandy scaldy soil, such as these parts of Suffolk, is one horse land. Roman auxiliary cavalrymen and their horses were known for their naturally close bonds, their having descended from 'barbarian' horsemen of the Steppes. The cavalrymen lived communally with his mount in *contubernia* (a cavalry barrack with wholly integrated stabling). This is not so differently from how the Horsemen of Suffolk lived, centuries later, with their shire plough teams.

Domestication *(to be pulled from the earth)* "wild plants are transformed into crops with altered morphologies, anatomies, physiologies and chemistries. Eventually, domesticated plants become dependent on us; they can no longer compete with other species outside cultivation". Source: https://herbaria.plants.ox.ac.uk/bol/plants400/Profiles/GH/Hordeum.

Seeing Blue *(how to stop so much water being lost from wheat ears)* blue light drives fast opening of stomata, wheat is very responsive to blue light so suffers high water loss. The removal of wheats ability, by genetic extraction, to see blue is an effort to try to stop so much water being lost from wheat ears and thus boost the green yield of the wheat crop. With special thanks to Professor Tracy Lawson, School of Life Sciences, University of Essex and her lecture "Take a breath: Stomal behaviour for optimising photosynthesis, water use and keeping cool" given at the Beth Chatto Education Trust symposium on 29 August 2024.

Collective motion, or winter grazing of a fresh field of vetch *(a force field)*; this poem responds to watching and passing the time of day with our local shepherd and having read a modelling and simulation feature in *Physicsworld* acknowledgement goes to the researchers and modellers into the physics of sheep at https://physicsworld.com/a/field-work-the-physicsof-sheep-from-phase-transitions-to-collective-motion (IOP Publishing, 26 September 2024)

R a v e n was inspired by its robotic counterpart as reported in 636, 86–91 (2024) in "Fast ground-to-air transition with avian-inspired multifunctional legs." by Shin, W.D., Phan, Nature HV., Daley, M.A. et al."

Acknowledgements and Thanks

First and Foremost, there aren't thanks deep or wide enough to convey to Tony for publishing my work yet again. It is an enormous honour to appear between covers anointed with the Shearsman logo, the true home of experimental poetry.

And to David Caddy for his prescience, for his understanding of the way of my work, for his care, courage and superb editorship and for supporting me from the very beginning.

And to Professor Chris McCully for knowing that land is time, and for recognising in his words, the 'lexical polychronicity' in *A Cranic of Ordinaries*, and so encouraging me on to this next collection. And for very nearly making me an angler. To you, for calling up the dragons, I dedicate *'I felt a funeral in my brain; in a dominating style, he was painted'*.

And to the following publications where some of the pieces in this collection first appeared, my sincere thanks for your approbation; *Shearsman magazine, Tears in the Fence, The Rialto*. 'Slip face' was long listed in the National Poetry Competition 2023. 'Swallow Holes' won First Prize, and 'I felt a funeral in my brain; in a dominating style, he was painted' was longlisted in OSP's annual poetry awards 2024.

And always to my Family (human and non-human, furry and feathered) for being my family, to my rock of a husband, to my precious siblings, to you all for actually and metaphorically accompanying me uncomplainingly through acres of mud to examine barley, ditches, withies, woods and hedges, for tracking down lost ponds, and for continually calibrating my microscope, mending my moth lights and for feeding the hedgehogs. I love you all.

www.ingramcontent.com/pod-product-compliance
Lightning Source LLC
Chambersburg PA
CBHW031633160426
43196CB00006B/400